CONFIDENCE, LOVE, RESPECT...

How to Deal with "I Don't Love You"

be in any fashion deemed liable for any hardship or damages that may befall them after undertaking information described herein.

Additionally, the information found on the following pages is intended for informational purposes only and should thus be considered, universal. As befitting its nature, the information presented is without assurance regarding its continued validity or interim quality. Trademarks that mentioned are done without written consent and can in no way be considered an endorsement from the trademark holder.

Table of Contents

INTRODUCTION

Thank you so much for purchasing the *Marriage Counseling Book: How to Deal with "I Don't Love You."*

The process of falling in love is like falling down a flight of stairs; it can be exciting, it can hurt, it can damage you but in ways that make you a better person. The beginning of loving relationships is created with a sprinkle of attraction, a dose of lust, and an overflowing cup of uncertainty. No one is certain if they will be with the person they are currently in a relationship with forever, but it is magical when the possibility of forever happens!

Marriage is a sacred act, the binding of two souls that have fallen in love and decided to weather life's storms and the sunshine that comes out afterward. Those that get married are typically very happy and are glad to finally officially connect with a piece of paper to their best friend.

But once the years start to fly by, that wonderful honeymoon stage wears off and the rocks that life throws at all once happily married couples begin to take its toll. When love starts to fade, so do the little things that couples once did for one another as well as other small things that make the entire establishment of marriages crumble.

With the crumbling of a relationship comes negative language to one another, possible cheating, broken trust and hurt feelings.

If you and your spouse are struggling to make ends meet in regard to your marriage, then you have made a good decision purchasing this book to get the valuable information you need in order to start rebuilding your foundation with your loved one, learn to forgive, regain respect and make the changes to yourself that are required to rebuild your marriage.

Thank you again for choosing this book to assist you, and your spouse get the peace, love, and respect back in your once loving marriage. These sorts of commitments are meant to last till death do you part. Why let the stress of everyday life ruin something so sacred when there are many easy fixes that you and your spouse can do? Every effort was made to ensure it is full of as much useful information as possible. I hope that you find the answers you need to stitch up old wounds and make new, loving memories with your partner.

CHAPTER 1

THE PROBLEM WITH MARRIAGE TODAY

It is no secret that there are many issues with modern marriages. We are living in a world where we see family breakdowns as the norm rather than the exception. Illegitimacy and divorce are becoming more widespread than ever before. Despite there being suggestions on ways to update the family model, there are many reasons that modern marriages are nothing less than dysfunctional. Is it any wonder that young adults are confused about marriage?

The life of married couples has drastically changed since the mid-1900's. Marriages used to be seen as a contract that was much more binding than it is today. Society used to have a crystal-clear view of what was acceptable and what generally worked well for successful family dynamics. Divorce was rare and frowned upon, especially by the church. When marriages were facing trouble, couples worked hard to hold those partnerships together. That simple phrase "Till death do us part" was not just a phrase but the first layer of bricks in a marital foundation. It meant everything back in the day.

Over the past few decades, the entire nature of marriage as totally changed. One of the biggest problems that marriages and families face is the face we have become much more approving of staying in long-term relationships without getting married. We somehow view in modern culture that living together is a better alternative to not becoming an added statistic in terms of the divorce rate. Many folks believe that a marriage license does nothing to constitute marriage. This means that without saying "I do" all these couples are taking on the responsibilities that married people have, such a paying bills and dividing household duties.

While many couples are blatantly deciding to skip marriage, there are many others that choose to live together before getting hitched, in an effort to get to know their spouse better. But there is a big problem with this approach. It leads to more divorces since avoiding divorce is a reason to cohabit, to begin with. In fact, the chance of divorce for couples that lived together before getting married is 50%.

So why in the world has the idea of marriage become so unappealing, unsatisfying, and unstable? Many blame it on how easy it is to get a divorce today compared to the past, while others say it is a decline in the desire to get married. Others would argue that there is a major decline in the respect that people have for the institution, even though many couples still express their desire to get married and are still hopeful for the change to create a happy union through the saying of "I do."

There have been many changes to the expectations we have for marriage as well, which set the perfect stage for them to fail and feel unsatisfying. Throughout history, we have expected our spouse to fulfill our needs for pertinent resources, such as food and income, safety and security, and the feeling of being loved. But in "modern marriage," we not only have the expectation for our spouse to facilitate our needs for connections but also to fulfill our needs to further grow and develop. While many couples have become less dependent on their partner for things such as a reliable source of income, we have now become more reliant than ever before on our spouse to meet our desperate need to feel positive self-actualization and self-esteem. In marriages today, our partners are expected to wear many hats, from cheerleaders, challengers, adventurers, confidants, best friends, etc. Plus, add the fact that many couples spend less time with family and friends and you will be able to see why so many start to view marriage as more of a burden than a partnership.

Another issue is that people these days are spending far less time than they should be on providing maintenance to their relationships. It is not a wonder that so many couples are left feeling unsatisfied and wildly disappointed in their marriages.

It is a fact that living within a successful and happy marriage in today's world is challenging. Many people set themselves up automatically to be disappointed, which quickly leads to divorce. Fortunately, there is hope! You have the power to change the way you view and treat your marriage in such modernized times. All it takes is a shift in attitude and actions. When you are able to fully understand the challenges that modern unions face, you are better equipped to combat issues that will inevitably arise.

CHAPTER 2

ISSUES THAT CAN EVEN THREATEN HAPPY MARRIAGES

No matter how hard you try, no one is capable of creating the perfect relationship. Relationships of all labels will not be free of issues all the time. Fruitful marriages take commitment, dedicated work, and reevaluation in the way we communicate, what we expect and what each partner needs to work on. But, we seem to make marriage a heck of a lot harder than it has to be. There are some very common issues that are found among hundreds of thousands of marriages that are more recurring than others.

The future of a marriage is highly dependent on how couples deal with problems that come about, which is why it is not only helpful but valuable to learn about the most common issues that marriages face today. This chapter covers the most prevalent problems that married couples have to face and how you can overcome them before it wrecks a great thing!

Boundary Overstepping

When people get married, more often than not you will find that there is always one of the partners putting extreme effort in changing their spouse. From fundamental beliefs to their sense of fashion, trying to change your partner to better fit your needs is a direct invasion of personal space. When you do this, you are victimizing your partner, which makes them feel hurt and disrespected and sometimes angry.

Overstepping over personal boundaries is usually done intentionally and with a mission in mind. This behavior literally steps all over the idea of having mutual respect for one another, and will eventually result in withdrawal. This behavior makes it difficult for couples to be open with one another and communicate effectively.

On the other hand, it can happen that you unintentionally overstep your spouse's boundaries at time, especially if you are in the process of sincerely attempting to help them. Know when to draw the line when it comes to making changes and pushing for them to avoid total invasion.

Talking versus Communicating

One of the most prominent issues in marriages is believing that talking is communicating, but this is a wrong mindset to have. Things such as complaining and emotional blackmail are not communicating but criticizing. Communicating in a poor manner can lead to major marital issues later down the line.

It is vital to realize that "talking" and "communicating" differ from one another greatly. Talking is providing information without the need for a response, which leaves the opportunity for criticism and complaint. Communicating is both a verbal and nonverbal exchange of information that requires responses. It takes more than one person to properly communicate since it is all about focusing on the connection between the people conversing.

Communication is an act where it should be okay to share ideas and information totally free of judgment.

When couples fail to communicate properly, it can be quite easy to make it a habit of ineffectively speaking to one another. If the poorness of communication is not dealt with, it can be a place for future problems to grow. Married folks should really learn how to communicate in order to keep their lives with one another on track and prevent the rising of unnecessary issues.

Decline of Sexual Intimacy

As the honeymoon phase of marriage wears off, life gets back to normal, and there are many reasons as to why couples might lose interest in intimacy from time to time. This is normal. But it is crucial that couples strive to find ways to keep their love life fulfilling and fresh. While sex is a small piece to the marital puzzle, it is unheard of to have a fruitful relationship without it.

Sadly, sex life tends to happen in a vicious cycle if left untouched for too long. It can be challenging to want to have sex when partners feel emotionally detached, but it can hard to feel that needed emotional attachment when there is no physical intimacy. To be able to get past dry spells, couples must be willing to seek out problem areas within the union and work through them to once again become comfortable with one another physically again.

Meandering Focuses

Another issue that many married couples face is a shift in their focus after the marriage is official. When one or both of the partners redirect their attention from the relationship to things such as their jobs, friends, children, hobbies, social activities, etc., it is natural for the other person in the marriage to feel a loss of attention. It is these situations where married folks may start to feel more like roommates than lovers.

It is crucial for both partners to find a balance of interests and the attention they provide their partner. It is encouraged for each people in unions to have their own goals and interests, as long as they are able to fit quality time in with one another.

The main reason this becomes an issue is that one or both parties tend to overreact, which makes both sides feel like they are unable to have a life without their spouse. Understand that your partner has won you, so now is a time to find the balance to grow the marriage as well as pursue other life challenges. Finding a happy medium will help your marriage to grow, as well as be strong enough to support the ambitions of one another.

Emotional Infidelity

It is a very common occurrence that once couples are married that they become emotionally disconnected and unengaged from one another. When this occurs, one or both spouse's needs become unmet, which naturally leads them to look elsewhere to fulfill them. This is where emotional infidelity can make its way into even the happiest of marriages.

Many couples often agree that emotional infidelity is more degrading than cheating physically because it involves much more than just sex, but also the connection with another person on many intimate levels.

To prevent this type of infidelity from happening in your marriage, you both need to be on the same page of what you consider to be "cheating." This will reduce the chance of allowing this to happen in the first place. It is also vital that couples remain tuned in to the emotional needs of one another. If needs are being properly fulfilled, there is no reason that either party should be interested in looking somewhere else.

Financial Disagreements

The bonding of two people also may include the partnering of bank accounts. Even if this is not the case, couples that keep their finances separate still face problems when it comes to finances.

Talking about money can be tense and highly stressful, especially if both partners have different habits with spending and managing their money. When it comes to communicating about finances, it is common for the conversation to be more about habits and personal values than money itself.

Ensure that you and your partner are on the same page when it comes to money and finances. Make it a priority to make a financial plan together so that you can wave any disagreements in the future.

Lack of Appreciation

Conflict feeds on the waning of appreciation in marriages. Both sexes crave recognition, so when couples cease to acknowledge the efforts of their partner, the other will stop those actions that were once appreciated and are now overseen. This can create bitter tension and agitation.

At the beginning of a marriage, both partners make it a priority to show their gratitude for their spouse with loving gestures. But once this stops, those once appreciated actions lose their magic and tend to be seen as a chore more than a choice. No matter how long you and your partner have been together, it is crucial to continue to show your appreciation for the things you both do for one another.

Addiction to Technology

The world today is highly dependent on technology usage, which makes it hard not to get caught up in our electronic devices. This is one of the biggest reasons why couples are reporting unhappiness in marriages these days.

When you begin to interact with friends by phone at the dinner table, you are ignoring your spouse. When you play on your tablet or computer after dinner instead of engaging with your spouse, you are replacing the opportunities for intimacy and healthy communication. If you allow it, technology does have a way of getting between marriages and literally taking it over. It is time to snap back to reality.

Selfishness

If one party in a union continuously puts their needs and desires ahead of their partner's, it is only a matter of time till the other spouse begins to feel unloved and unworthy of their spouse's love. Marriage is built on the foundation of promising to love one another for better or worse. A portion of this promise is to not act in selfish ways. Sounds easy, right?

Despite our best efforts, there are times that selfishness comes in various forms that we fail to recognize right away. Selfishness is a monster that is abusive, possessive, jealous, manipulative and heavily controlling. To opposing parties, it can be seen as disrespect and a lack of consideration.

To prevent selfishness from coming between you and your spouse, each side must learn how to engage with empathy and build a balance to ensure both partners are getting what they need from the marriage.

Lack of Trust

It is safe to say that without trust there is truly no love. It is what makes up a big portion of the foundation of all love, especially in a marriage. Healthy marriages do not exist without trust. When a partner breaks a promise, lies, or cheats, it can drastically hurt or even kill the relationship.

It is not easy to restore trust, and takes commitment from both partners to fix the relationship in order to fulfill prosperity in the union again. If issues are not dealt with they are left to fester, which can cause the betrayed spouse to feel suspicious of the other's actions, angry, and hurt.

The Changes of Future Ambitions

When couples go to get married, they are often on the same page and path with what they want for their futures. The reason this is such a common issue is that life brings about changes and one or both partners change their minds and start to fulfill new ambitions. This is why it is vital to keep lines of communication open so that if one or both of you do change your mind, you can avoid the change in ambitions from being a shocking awakening to your partner.

Inability to Forgive

One of the biggest roots of problematic issues in marriages is the lack of willingness or the total inability to forgive each other. From petty to traumatic offenses,

90% of the issues within partnerships are due to the inability to forgive themselves, their spouse, or other people that have impacted their lives in negative ways.

No worries, there is an entire chapter dedicated to forgiveness. Even the most intense of problems can be properly forgiven over time.

Within the remaining chapters of this book, you will find valuable insight, information, tips, methods, and techniques on how you can revive that once beautiful spark between you and your spouse!

CHAPTER 3

SIGNS YOUR MARRIAGE IS IN TROUBLE

One of the most painful things in life is seeing the disintegration of a once loving marriage. It is one of the worst emotionally, mentally, and physically painful things you may ever experience in your lifetime.

Instead of accepting defeat and wrecking an aspect of your life that you wanted to be around "Till death do you part," we will start the mending of your marriage by discussing some warning signs that you might be aware of or you have yet to take notice of.

Arguing about same subjects

All marriages inevitably face challenges and disputes from time to time, but if you find that you and your partner are constantly bantering about the same subjects on a regular occasion, this could be a major red flag. If you continuously are unable to find a compromise to agree to disagree, then you will both constantly struggle to maintain a strong relationship.

Constantly saying ugly things to one another

Always thinking with an argumentative tone to one another is mean and leads to hurt feelings. In fact, contempt is the number one predictor of a path being paved towards divorce. Negative and sly commentary, hostile remarks, teasing, sarcasm, teasing, mocking and disrespectful words, as well as negative body language all, lead to the poisoning of marriages.

No responsibility taken

One of the main things that put your marriage automatically on the rocks is when neither side takes responsibility for their actions or fails to acknowledge their faults.

When people take responsibility during disagreements, this shows a willingness to do what needs to be done in order to save the marriage.

Different intimacy views

If the lines of communication seem to be closed off, then this could mean double trouble for the marriage. When communication is cut off, this eventually leads to a sexless and unpassionate marriage. You must let your spouse know what your needs are and vice versa.

Constant suspicion of one another

A partnership without trust will never last. It is what makes the foundation for all kinds of relationships in our lives stable and healthy. You marriage will incvitably struggle if you are always wondering if your partner has your best interest in mind and will never do anything to deceive or hurt you.

No longer go on dates

Ask yourself how long you have had one-on-one time with your spouse, time without any distractions? Five minutes, an hour, perhaps less? If you and your spouse no longer spend quality time together without distractions, you should make it a top priority to make each other a priority in your lives.

Happier and content being apart than with each other

Marriages that are healthy involve two people that genuinely like spending quality time with one another. If you or your spouse find that you are happier away from each other than when you are together, then there are some underlying problems that have the potential to shake things up in your marriage negatively. Time spent together is needed to develop both physical and emotional connections that are crucial to a healthy and happy partnership.

Dishonesty about finances

Like you have read several times before already, relationships without trust and transparency is like trying to drive to a destination without any gas. You will only sit in the car, but fail to go anywhere. Even if you push and shove that car, you will not get far whatsoever. If you or your spouse lies, hides, or gambles away your money, don't hesitate to confront them about the issue. You need to have peace of mind that your spouse has your back and is willing, to be honest with you no matter what.

Cannot agree on compromises

If neither party in a marriage is unable to find compromise in order to solve issues, this will eventually result in hefty escalations. You will find that over time your fights grow more intense and tend to hurt worse. If you find yourself trying to keep your head above water when it comes to finding a balance, continue speaking in a respectful manner to one another till you both can find a solution you can both feel content with.

Don't allow one another time to spend with others

Your marriage is in trouble if you find that your spouse fails to let you spend time with family, friends, co-workers and other people. Healthy marriages have no place for possessive behavior.

Thoughts about being unfaithful

Even having an inkling of being unfaithful can be a cause for major trouble. It is not okay for either party to let eyes wander to other people. You should only seek excitement within your marriage and never from other external sources.

Flirting online

If either party in a marriage flirts with others online, then it is likely that the marriage is unstable. Even if you have never met or plan to meet the people you are talking to via the internet, your thoughts that are devoted to people other than your spouse can be greatly considered as an emotional affair.

Only communication being superficial topics

If you find that the only conversations you have with your spouse are trivial in nature, it can be a very bad sign. Healthy marriages have conversations that do much more than scratch the surface of the real thoughts and feelings both parties have. Open communication is a fantastic way to feel connected with your spouse on an intellectual and emotional level. Make it a priority to discuss feelings, concerns, ambitions, and goals. This is a key to a long-lasting marriage.

Feeling of worthlessness

If you find that criticism is always coming between you and your spouse, this could mean trouble. It's vital for each spouse to have the confidence that they have your back and are there to support you. Don't allow yourself to be a partner's doormat. You should never feel patronized or belittled. If you constantly feel like you are not enough for your spouse, take the time to talk to them to get to the core of the issue.

Shame on one another

Having disgust and shame towards each other should not be allowed in any marriage. Accusations against the character and intentions of your spouse are harmful to your willingness to sustain a lasting partnership.

Feeling of loneliness even when spouse is present

If you feel lonely even when your partner is sitting right next to you, this means that there is more than likely a lack of connection between you and your spouse. Make it a priority to cultivate a marriage of not only a friendship but of deep connection.

Make decisions based on yourself

At the beginning of a marriage, you find that you ask your partner for their opinion, point of view, and expertise on various subjects. It is when you find yourself making decisions without considering the feelings of your spouse or how it may affect them that trouble starts.

Being tallying

If you are finding that you and your spouse are constantly keeping tally and keeping a conscious mental note on how much you contribute to the marriage, this can be a cause for major agitation.

Teammates to roommates

Teammates work together to accomplish goals, sharing ideas on how they can succeed and envision their lives, home, and plans together. Roommates, however, act on singular projects with no thought or act of respect towards one another. They take care of their own space, acting out on separate plans, which eventually become their separate lives.

Removal of knives in the back to hurt one another

Those who have been in relationships with another human being long enough are consciously aware of the buttons they do not like being pushed. You have found ways to avoid pushing those buttons. But, as a marriage wears on, you find that you intentionally press them and actually like pestering them.

Call yourself king or queen of the home

In a fruitful marriage, no needs are more important than others. The desires of two people are split equally and you both attempt to fulfill one another's needs. But as life goes on, stress and resentment can cause tension, making you feel like your needs and desires take priority.

Immediate family chooses sides instead of fighting for common ground

You will find that with miscommunication and disrespect are right alongside with your immediate family members choosing to pick "upsides" during conversations and debates. The matter of winning or losing becomes the mission instead of shooting for compromise. This leads to both you and your spouse isolating one another from friends and family.

One of the worst things that can happen is letting your marriage become just as dysfunctional as the display of division between the lack of misunderstanding among family members. The unity of family disintegrates, which leads to major family feuds, which is terrible for any sort of healthy marriage.

CHAPTER 4

REBUILDING YOUR MARRIAGE AFTER AN AFFAIR

There are few to no marital issues that cause as much devastation and heartache as infidelity, an action that totally undermines the foundation of the sanctity of marriage. Cheating can bring about damaging consequences to a married couple and is more often than not a deal breaker that results in a divorce. But there are many couples that decide to weather out the aftermath of hurricane infidelity rather than part ways.

Understanding Infidelity

Adultery cannot be defined by a clear or single situation. In fact, what is considered as cheating varies greatly among couples. Is an emotional connection with no physical ties with someone outside the marriage considered cheating? What about relationships with people online? Every person and couple need to clearly communicate what they individually and together consider to be infidelity within their marriage.

Reasons Affairs Occur

There is a plethora of factors that can contribute to the happening of infidelity and surprisingly, many have nothing to do with sexual intimacy.

- Marital issues that have been left unaddressed for years

- Addiction to alcohol, drugs, gambling, sex, etc.

- Mental health problems like bipolar disorder, learning disabilities, ADD, anxiety, depression, etc.

- Physical health problems, such as disability or chronic pain

- Communication breakdowns that are caused by emotional and needs of the relationship

- Reduction of fondness

- Loss of caring for one another

- Lack of overall affection

The Discovery of an Affair

When one initially discovers that an affair has been happening behind their back, it can trigger very powerful emotions for both partners in the marriage. Emotions such as remorse, guilt, depression, shame, anger, and betrayal can create an ugly head between a couple. It can be challenging to think clearly in order to make decisions that decide the long-term of a marriage. Here are a few things to consider:

- <u>Don't be rash</u>: If you think that the buildup of emotions might lead to you physically hurting yourself, your partner, or anyone else, seek professional assistance right away.

- <u>Provide space</u>: Finding out about affairs is intense. You will find yourself thinking erratic thoughts and feel very unlike yourself as you try to grasp the severity of what has occurred. Avoid intense discussions so you can begin the mending process.

- <u>Find support</u>: Find trusted loved ones and/or friends that you can share your feelings and experience with. Find people who will support, encourage, and help you through the healing process. Avoid those who you think will be biased, critical, or too judgmental. Spiritual leaders might be a good place to start since they are trained and have experience with marriage issues.

- <u>Don't rush:</u> You may have a very deep need to understand what has happened in your marriage, but you must do your best to not dive into intimate details of the affair. Do so only with professional guidance. Otherwise, you might totally burn what is left of the bridge between you and your partner.

Steps to Mending a Marriage After an Affair

The process of mending after cheating or emotional infidelity doesn't happen quickly. Even those that are dedicated to making things work after the fact end up with waylaid feelings, resentment, and guilt that paralyzes.

For the person who cheated, it is natural to think things like "How did I get here?" or "I didn't see this coming…" No matter what exactly led you down the path to being unfaithful, there will come a point where it is time to wake-up, face the music and acknowledge what happened, especially how devastating your choices can be.

If you and your partner desire to pursue the healing process after infidelity, here are vital steps to take in order to emerge as an even stronger couple in your marriage after an affair.

- **End the Affair**

The one who cheated needs to cease all contact with the person they were unfaithful with. No quick meet-ups, phone calls, texts, and especially no romantic or sexual contact. If the other person does make contact, tell your spouse about it before they ask. This is the first step to rebuilding trust in the marriage.

- **Be Honest**

For many people on the other side of cheating, they need the wronged spouse to spew into detail about the affair. It is also crucial that the hurt partner feels heard, especially since it is easy to feel like they are crazy when grieving. When they ask you about the affair, be brutally honest. This might bring about more pain at first, but it will help later down the line as you mend your relationship. This might seem very counterintuitive, but it is vital in order to rebuild trust. Tell them the entire truth about the affair and be as transparent as possible. Explain to them how it came about and how you ended it. This gives the hurt spouse a timeline to feel confident that you are no longer hiding secrets from them. Be totally open to them asking you questions that pertain to your whereabouts. Transparency is crucial to the mending process.

Protect Your Spouse from Sexual Details

Although total transparency is critical to being honest, giving away too many details in regard to the sexual intimacy of the affair will give your spouse images that they do not need to think about. If you must, seek the help of a counselor to walk you through this process. They will be able to decipher information that is useful and what is hurtful.

Take Responsibility

Along with honesty comes taking total responsibility for the affair. Even though there were probably underlying issues in the marriage that initiated the seeking of infidelity, the cheating spouse was the one who acted upon it. They betrayed the vows of marriage, despite the issues in it. It is very easy to slide right into the game of blame, but a vital step is knowing the choice you made and putting excuses and scapegoats to the side.

Empathize and Bear Witness to the Hurt Partner

It is natural for the hurt party to have emotional responses to your act of unfaithfulness. In order to mend together, you must be willing to seek how it must feel to be the betrayed spouse. This is no time to demand that they own their faults that might have caused you to make poor decisions. At this point, you must establish the commitment you have to the marriage.

Being empathetic can lead to heartfelt forgiveness. In fact, one of the best indicators that your marriage will survive this fallout is if the unfaithful partner shows empathy towards the one they betrayed.

Yes, it is also natural for the unfaithful spouse to want to fight back to defend their reasoning, but there is no place for that at this point. They must sit back and try to understand how their spouse feels. Validate their pain by showing tenderness and compassion. Understand the choices you made have caused a great deal of turmoil in your marriage. It is challenging, but allow them as much space and time as they need to process the deep tides of emotions they are feeling and respond to their woes with regret and honesty.

Make the Commitment to Recommit to Your Spouse

Clarify to your spouse that you are dedicated to fight for your marriage. You have deeply burned the bridge of trust between the two of you and realize that rebuilding it will take time. The steps you take now must be proactive, which is crucial to the recovery of your relationship.

Write an Apology

Once the cheating spouse has listened and understood their partner's declaration of their emotionally-fueled feelings, it is recommended by many professionals that the cheater writes out the account in their own words. Writing a less that gives details and specific points proves that they do grasp the sorrow they have caused thanks to their actions. Don't use "I'm sorry" a lot, it won't get you far. Use verbal reassurances and make promises that something this detrimental won't occur again. A written apology must prove that they have taken the time to understand what the hurt spouse is feeling. This means citing examples of how they have hurt their spouse and taking actions to prove that it will not happen again in the future.

Avoid "Cheap Forgiveness"

The desire to salvage the marriage after infidelity can be overwhelming, which can cause the need to vent anger to be pushed to the side. The wronged partner then forgives their unfaithful spouse before they have a chance to seethe. This behavior does more harm than good and is seen often in people who are simply scared of being alone rather than the consequences of forgiving a cheating partner too soon. "Cheap forgiveness" not only swindles the wronged partner from undergoing the grieving process, but it sets up the relationship to experience future infidelities when they do not force their spouse to grasp the pain they have caused.

Share the Responsibility

Infidelity (usually) occurs with only one partner in the marriage. Even though it is the fault of one person for acting unfaithfully, there are oftentimes reasons that both parties of a marriage hold blame for cheating occurring. The one who was unfaithful should own up to 100% of their guilt since no one forced them to cheat, but the wronged spouse should also acknowledge how they played a role in fostering this to happen. It is important that both partners must see how they had a hand in creating the isolation and loneliness that compelled their spouse to seek intimacy elsewhere.

Set Boundaries and Rules

To allow the marriage to recover from the blow of infidelity, there must be ways to grant and earn trust back. Establish rules that are non-negotiable at the very start of the healing process. It can include things such as:

- The wronged spouse requesting that their spouse always answer their phone, even if they are in a place that a full conversation cannot be had

- If infidelity happened online, the hurt spouse could make a rule to look over their partner's shoulder when they are on the computer.

Though these sounds a little unorthodox, bringing an imbalance of power eases the insecure feelings and the mistrust that the hurt party has. It also proves that the cheating partner is willing to give up their right to privacy while their partner regains the confidence in their marriage.

Healing of the Cheater's Heart

Even though the spouse who was unfaithful was in the wrong, they will also experience a world of emotion. From unworthiness, guilt, and shame, these negative emotions can keep the marriage from the healthy mending it needs to survive. Marriages that last are made up of two healthy individuals. So the cheater may need outside help in order to become healthier mentally to partake in the sustainability of a long-lasting marriage after infidelity.

Express Gratitude

If you have made it this far in married life after infidelity, then you know that the wronged spouse is fighting to keep the marriage despite the cheater's past choices. This is an act of a sacrificial love, which means you should be showing major actions of how grateful you are that they love you enough to keep you around.

Redefine Sexual Intimacy

After dealing with the hurricane of emotions, the next biggest hurdle in healing a marriage after an affair lies between the sheets. It often feels as though the person your partner cheated with is lying right in-between you, a ghost that strains sexual relations.

This can mean major trouble in this aspect of the marriage. The spouse that was unfaithful may feel pressured to please their partner, which leads to low-performance thanks to distraction. Then the hurt partner, who is already heavily insecure, interprets the low performance as a lack of attraction and interest.

Remember that it takes time to regain the passion that your marriage once had, especially after infidelity. It's important to express desires and fears, which eventually will lead to vulnerability in a physical manner, which can foster sexual intimacy.

Ignore Common Perceptions of Cheaters

We frequently hear the phrase, "once a cheater, always a cheater." This assumption is dangerous in terms of rebuilding a marriage. Plus, many people who have cheated think that because of perceptions like this, that they may be susceptible of cheating on their spouse again in the future. Inevitably, there will be folks that cheat again. But remember that there are people that act upon it once and never think about doing it again. They have learned their lesson.

This being said, while you should ignore common aphorisms, it is vital to remember that if the adulterer is not willing to listen to the hurt spouse speak of their experience with the pain of infidelity, it may be a red flag that it is not worth the time and effort it takes to rebuild trust.

Reality Check

The aftermath of hurricane infidelity can lead to the feeling that a marriage is dysfunctional. A unique point of view is to remember that many long-term couples experience at least one instance of infidelity in some form or another and manage to make it through. The stigma of adultery keeps this rising issue on the DL, but despite the negativity that surrounds the marriage after the fact, there are numerous couples that come out of an affair closer and more honest than they were before!

Marriages can greatly benefit from trust-building and emotional closures, no matter if it is infidelity or something else that sparks this crucial development.

Letting Go

It's important to remember that healing a marriage after infidelity not only takes the opening up of the cheater but of the spouse that was hurt by this experience as well. The wronged partner must be willing to loosen the leash of pain over time and allow the trust to grow. The restoration of a marriage relies on both parties to prove that they are willing to put new energy into the relationship. This requires both partners to take risks. It is also pertinent to remember that this process takes time. There will be days that it feels like the two of your make leaps and bounds, while other days you feel that you both are pushed back to square one.

Affairs give marriages major shock waves for months to years. But it is more than possible to restore and totally rebuild the marriage to be greater than it was before infidelity occurred. The road to recovery is anything but easy, but if you are both it in for the long haul, it can be an unexpected gift that your marriage needed all along. If you both push through it, a stronger, better union can emerge.

Mistakes in Rebuilding Marriages

Infidelity is a total violation of boundaries in a relationship. Therefore, many people think that imposing tighter restrictions and boundaries to prevent it from happening again seem like the way to go. But this is by no means effective in the long run. Why? Because affairs don't just occur in bad marriages. They can happen in good ones too. This means infidelity is not the problem, but rather just a symptom of the real issue.

When marriages are faced with cheating, two common questions are asked:

1. *What went wrong to make this happen?*

2. *Why did I not see this coming?*

These are natural, but then to fix what is wrong and to prevent it from happening again, many couples make one of these mistakes:

1. They overcorrect by being too controlling

2. They overcompensate by changing too much

Obviously, both of these approaches can majorly back-fire. Why? Because affairs can be usually attributed to four key things, also known as the 'ABC's of Infidelity.'

Before we talk about these ABC's, I want to introduce you to something referred to as "The Broken Windows Theory." It represents that having a broken window in your home would make it much more likely for someone to break in with ease, even though a window is not a cause for a break in. This is the same logic that applies to the ABC's of Infidelity.

There are four specific things that make a marriage vulnerable to cheating:

- **A** represents *"attention,"* or therefore heavily lacking. It can make people very vulnerable to temptations.

- **B** represents *"boredom,"* or couples in a marriage taking things for granted. A lack of newness in a relationship is a main reason why affairs occur, rather than a lack of love. Even the best of relationships are not immune to boredom.

- **C** represents too much *"control."* Either partner being too controlling can be perceived by both as a major lack of freedom in a marriage, which makes people more likely to rebel against one another. This is why so many affairs are based on revenge.

- **C** represents not enough *"communication,"* which can easily create rifts in a marriage of any kind.

Mistake #1: Over-correction by too much control

Let's take it a step further and consider how infidelity could be a way that a spouse controls the other. We all have hard-wired needs, one of the biggest being the need for self-expression and freedom. Freedom to some is seen as just an American value when really it is a human *need.* We all desire the freedom to express our individuality, the freedom to say no, to choose, and to change our minds.

The issue is, however, that it can be rather challenging to balance the need for free with our need for safety. In an effort to make these needs meet, couples suffocate one another. This is the beginning of the stifling of each other's independence.

We can sit there and imagine and think that is it possible to control another person, but in reality, it's not. You are able to control people as much as you are capable of controlling the weather, which is not at all. In an effort to create safety, all that controlling often just lead to rebellion and stagnation. This means it's only a matter of time before each spouse resents one another.

Even if you have the best of intentions, trying your hardest to create a safety net within your marriage often leads to an excessive amount of control that leads to the breaking of those windows we spoke about earlier. This means that many affairs are simply an act of rebellion, a spouse's moment of defiance, or a passive-aggressive way to push against the feeling of being too controlled. Control of any kind doesn't make security, but rather compliance. Defiance lurks right underneath compliance. So, remember this rule if you want to avoid falling into this controlling trap:

Rule #1: Fidelity is a choice <u>and</u> a commitment that cannot be forced or enforced.

The bad news is your spouse will be faithful by choice. This means you cannot demand their loyalty to you. All you can do is *inspire* it. The good news? There *is* a lot you can do to inspire this type of fidelity and devotion in your marriage. Shift focus from attempting to control and learn ways to rekindle the desire within one another. This is the way to instill loyalty, monogamy, and faithfulness for life.

Mistake #2: Overcompensation by too much change

This mistake is a classic one that is created by a lack of knowledge of what exactly went wrong to lead to an affair. Couples tend to make the assumption that everything was wrong, therefore, making way too many changes all at once in an effort to create something new from the crumbled marriage after Hurricane Affair.

I am sure you have heard of 'open marriages,' where couples agree to go against the tradition of monogamy and give one another permission to engage in extramarital affairs. Is this better in terms of preventing infidelity than traditional rules of a monogamous marriage? You may be surprised to find out that both open and traditional marriages are susceptible to adultery. Why? Because any sort of partnership relies heavily on transparency and honesty. Deception is the enemy in both of these types of marriages.

So, *is* there a way to have the benefits of monogamy while taking advantage of the adventure and novelty that open marriages offer? Yes, there is! Which leads us to the other rule:

Rule #2: Strong marriages are not created by default, but rather by design.

Customizing your marriage will help you and your spouse to keep the traditional boundaries you desire intact, while still leaving room for spontaneity, newness, and expansion. It is not all about making changes but making the right changes. While you should never ignore the things that might make your vulnerable, you should also not overreact either. Corrections and adjustments need to be made, but be mindful of them so that you are not overcompensating or correcting the situation by acting upon the wrong things and making the affair situation worse.

Sit down with your partner and discuss the kinds of changes you both would like to see. This will help to decipher the things you both value in a relationship. This means taking the time to ask those tough questions and making a dedicated effort to customize the rules to fit into *your* marriage.

CHAPTER 5

UNEXPECTED WAYS TO IMPROVE YOUR MARRIAGE

It's no secret that it takes two loving people to become a couple, fall in love, and say "I do." But when it comes to bettering the relationship, it only takes one person. If you are constantly waiting for your spouse to take the reins to better your marriage, then you are responsible for helping cook a recipe for unhappiness that may lead to divorce.

There are many things you can do every day to improve your marriage, which can be looking at yourself and changing your own behavior. This chapter brings to light unique methods of saving your marriage.

If you are in a marriage where the both of you have the basics covered, there are other things you can do to make it last effectively through the wear and tear of the years to come. All of these methods are ways to provide a spark and improve the overall quality of your marriage.

Ignore experts

While this might seem quite counterintuitive, you would be surprised just how effective thinking about what makes your spouse happy can really do to improve your relationship. Instead of seeking out an expert for advice and spending hundreds of dollars of your hard-earned money, start doing the things that make your spouse smile or will delight them. From cleaning trash out of the car to taking the chore of waking the kids up, start doing them now!

Invent an imaginary houseguest

When you have family, friends, or other guests at your home, you tend to think and act differently with your partner than usual, especially when you disagree. Take advantage of this fact next time you want to scream at one another. Imagine someone is staying in the room next to yours. This will help you to both think deeper about what you want to say and surprisingly relieve some tension that arguments create. This will encourage you to be more kind to your spouse, even when they have done something to upset you.

Stop correcting unrelated errors

There is no reason to dwell on things your spouse does wrong to the point of bringing up factors that make no difference. For example, it simply does not matter if there were 50 or 75 guests at a wedding when you are discussing that they have too much to drink.

Praise and love specifically

Saying things like, "You are so awesome, and I love you" is not necessarily a bad thing, but it could be more sufficient. Think back to the early days of your relationship with your partner. This is where you will find the qualities that attracted you to them in the first place. But the longer people are together, the less likely they are to mention these details that once meant the world to them.

Think about how specific your daily criticisms are, such as "Why did you put so much water in this pot?" or "You came home with six bananas when I just needed three!". Use that the tendency to be specific for when you praise your partner as well.

Put limits on listening

Listening is one of the best gifts you can give one another in any kind of relationship. It is something that many of us do not do enough of. However, there are times that a limit should be put to listening. There are times that you are doing so many things at once, from watching the kids to cooking to watching the news all at once, that sincerely listening to your partner as they try to speak to you about something simply doesn't work. Articulate a quick and calm sentence to inform them that you will be happy to listen to them later, such as "I am super busy right now, but will be happy to talk later."

Don't use the word 'foreplay'

All couples, married or not, need to make it a priority to talk about sex. But that is no reason to bring back "The

Joy of Sex" '70's vocabulary. Terms like 'foreplay' are not sexy. It also suggests that anything you do besides sex is not a real thing, and any other actions are just something you do to get ready for the act of sex.

Invite what you dread

If you are tired of hearing your spouse continuously talk about how worried they are about their mom in the nursing home, perhaps it is time that you start up the conversation. It is natural to worry that you might open up emotional wounds with your partner, but there are times that you must be willing to talk about subjects you dread. You will find though that your spouse worries less about these sorts of issues if they see that you are ready to invite them to tell you everything all in one moment. You do not have to be their cheerleader, but just be a good listener.

Use 'I-statement' wisely

The technique of using I-statements requires one to talk about how they feel instead of just what your partner feels. For example, if your spouse is late on a regular basis, instead of saying "It's rude that you are always late," say something like, "It's hard for me to plan dinner when you are late." This opens up a healthier discussion since it does not sound like you are attacking them. Just an FYI, not all I-statements mean that you are referring to yourself. Just remember to avoid commentary like, "I think you are controlling" unless you are looking to start a fight.

Disorient with praise

Instead of fulfilling your spouse's expectations that you will criticize them, surprise them with praise instead. For example, if they have a tendency, if they are often overbearing with their younger sibling and this is something you have previously fought over, say something such as, "I admire your humor with your brother. It lightens things up, and you are so funny with him." This is unexpected as well as disarming, which encourages new behavior from both parties in a marriage.

Describe with less

When a spouse says that they do not wish to talk or are not good at talking, the real issue usually is they get totally overwhelmed with too much information all at once. For example, instead of going off about multiple things at once, cut off at your point. "You told me you would clean up the kitchen and you haven't." Don't bother tacking on all those other issues you have with them at the moment.

Have secrets

Good and open communication is vital to a healthy marriage, but so is keeping certain things to yourself as well. For instance, if you start to get a small crush on a new coworker at the office, don't mention it to your partner. Or if you have your own bank account, they do not need to know how much you spent on that new gadget. You will both be more content if you do not mention these tiny, innocent discrepancies.

Tell lies

Honesty is the best policy, but there are some circumstances that lying will benefit the relationship. Don't blatantly tell your partner "yes" if they ask if they look fat when trying on an outfit. There are times that giving your spouse an ego boost is much more important than the truth.

Don't share

It is crucial to talk to your spouse about your interests, ideas, dreams, plans and about the day you had. But it is not necessary to tell them every single detail or thought you had. No one likes to listen to someone go on and on about the minute detail of a boring workday. If you are someone that finds themselves complaining a lot, this kind of sharing only bring your spouse down. Unless you are having an extremely bad day, do not overload your partner with your frustrations.

Have separate lives

This does not mean going out and starting a secret family. Spending time together is important, but there is such a thing as being together too much. The more time you spend with each other, the less you experience alone, and the less you have to tell your spouse. Neediness and dependence on a partner are wildly unattractive, but the opposite is true about people with a degree of independence. Have your own hobbies, interests, and friends. This will help to keep a spark of interest and the attraction you have for one another alive.

Be selfish

Keeping the spark of love alive takes compromise, tolerance, and patience. None of that is a bad thing! But this does not mean that you should give up on your own needs. While it may feel good to compromise all the time or for your spouse to have their own way, they will lose respect for you over time if you continue to be a doormat, especially if you are unhappy deep down. For the sake of your marriage, learn to be selfish on occasion.

Be irresponsible

Responsibilities, like paying the bills and taking care of the kids, is important, but it's equally as crucial to take

time to shake off worries and cares and act like a teen-
ager again. Do something a bit crazy with your partner
encourages the creation of new memories that will keep
you going when life gets serious. This is especially important to do while you are still young and capable of
getting into a bit of mischief.

Forego Valentine's Day

Learn early on how your spouse feels about holidays like
Valentine's Day. It is a safe bet to still have a backup
plan if they expect something, but if you are like me, I
strongly dislike the commercialism and consumerism of
the holiday. Discuss it and make a pact if you can to ignore the holiday. Laugh and wish one another a happy
Valentine's Day, but make the love you have for one another really count the other 364 days of the year. Romantic gestures are a great thing, but you should show your
spouse that you love them each and every day. You can't
just buy a pricey gift one day out of the year to make up
for the other days of ignoring them.

CHAPTER 6

BRINGING LOVE BACK INTO YOUR MARRIAGE

After you have been married to your partner for a while, you find that the majority of your conversations are centered around the kids, chores, work and other mundane aspects of everyday life. With the hustle, bustle and endless stress of day to day responsibilities, it can be challenging to keep the same loving feelings you both felt when you said, "I do" intact.

One of the biggest reasons that couples lose their passion is because of a 'pursuer-distancer' patterns that seem to naturally take place over time. This is a demand-withdraw pattern where one spouse becomes too aggressive and/or critical, and the other typically becomes distance and defensive. There are many couples that get stuck in this detrimental pattern. It has been shown that 80% of these couples get divorced within their first 4-5 years of living the married life.

It is nearly impossible and otherwise irresponsible to go on impromptu vacations or skip performing responsibilities to spend hours in bed. But there are some other exciting and fun techniques that are successful in bringing back the spark into your marriage. Make it a priority to challenge yourself to fall back in love with your spouse with the unique and fun methods outlined in this chapter!

Ways to Rekindle Sexual Passion

Promote emotional intimacy

All sexually healthy relationships are founded upon closeness. If you want to improve the physical aspects of your marriage, you must be willing to work on strengthening your emotional connection with your spouse. Focus on not only meeting the needs of your partner but effectively communicating your own needs in a respectful way.

If you are looking to add a spark to the passion that you once had, you must remember to turn towards one another. Practice emotional attunement in order to stay connected, even in times of disagreement. This means you must tune in to one another by a show of empathy rather than becoming defensive. Both spouses should speak about the way they feel in a positive way.

The expressing of positive needs is a part of the recipe needed for a successful and long-lasting partnership for both the speaker and the listener. This is because it conveys requests as well as complaints without blame and criticism. This means both parties will have to be willing to do the work in order to mentally transform their thoughts of what is wrong with one another to what they can provide to one another.

Revive intimate chemistry

During the first phases of marriage, couples are excited about falling in love. However, this state of bliss eventually fades. Science and the natural functioning of our bodies have a lot to do with this. At the beginning of relationships, the bonding hormone, oxytocin is released, causing infatuation that makes both parties feel turned on by touch and somewhat euphoric. Like a drug, it gives partners an immediate reward which also helps us to feel bonded to them.

Hugs, hand holding, and other tender touches are fantastic ways to reaffirm your love for your spouse. Physical affection is part of setting the stage for sexual pleasure. Set a goal to double the time you spend performing sensual touches, hugging and kissing, especially if you are looking to improve your marriage.

Sexual attraction is certainly not easily maintained over time. Many lose this passion because both sides are not willing to give up the control they have and show their vulnerable side. Many other sexual concerns are born from interpersonal issues within the marriage itself.

Change the way sex is initiated

Avoid playing the blame game and learn to mix things up in order to end the power struggle. Those who are distancers should practice initiating sex and those that play the role of pursuer should find ways to tell their spouse how sexy they are without the demand of being close.

Hold hands more

Even the simplest of touches like hugging and holding hands releases oxytocin, which then causing a sensation of calmness. It is also released during sexual orgasm as well. Physical affection helps to reduce hormones caused by stress. So why not hold those beautiful hands more?

Let tension build

Believe it or not, we experience much more pleasure when the anticipation of receiving an award is played out for a longer time. Take your sweet time during foreplay; change up locations where you have sex, make it more romantic, and even share each other's sexual fantasies.

Separate time for intimacy from the usual routine

Plan to be intimate and make it a point to not discuss issues within your marriage and everyday things like chores and the kids while in the bedroom. Arousal plummets when we are stressed out and distracted.

Make time to spend with your spouse

Dates are not just for teenagers! Carve out time to court and flirt with your spouse. This helps to initiate sexual intimacy. Also, try out new activities that bring both of you pleasure. In fact, everything you strive to do positively in your marriage each day impacts foreplay.

Hone in on affectionate touches

Give your spouse a back/shoulder rub, hold hands while watching a movie, gently caress their body with your fingertips, etc. Foreplay is associated with sexual intercourse, but affectionate touches are a very powerful way to show your spouse the passion you have for them. It helps to rekindle passion, even in partners that are not huge touchy-feely people.

Practice emotional vulnerability

Learn the importance of openly sharing your desires, fantasies and innermost wishes with your partner, both in bed and in everyday life.

Maintain curiosity

Don't be afraid to try out new ways to bring pleasure to your partner and vice versa. View sex as a time to get to know your spouse better time after time.

Mix up sex

Don't have just one kind of sex all the time, this will become rather boring after a while. Instead, aim to have highly erotic sex one night, more intimate another time, and gentle and tender sex on another occasion. This breaks up the routine and allows you to try new things as your sexual needs and desires change.

Easy Ways to Upgrade Your Marriage

Making your marriage more intimate, connected and secure shouldn't have to be overwhelming. Here are some great tips that lead to reaping the rewards much sooner than you think, while also building a stronger foundation in the long run.

Go to bed together

Sleeping together is both sexy and exciting when you first start dating your partner. But over time and after years of being married, you find that you go to bed at different times or may even sleep in separate beds. Any of these types of things can become a negative routine that you fall into. Going to bed together is something sacred that you only share with your partner. It shouldn't just be about sex, but rather a time that you can have a few intimate moments with them before catching some shuteye. It helps to align your schedules and feel more connected through the act of catching up. Make your bedroom free of cellular devices too, so both of you can be consciously present with one another before shutting out the lights.

Show your love

Love is not just a feeling, but rather a showing of feeling. As time goes on, it takes more effort to show how much you love your spouse. Even the littlest of things can go a long way! Write your partner a quick note, give them a foot rub, hold hands as you walk, pick up their favorite dessert, etc. The little things really add up over time. It shows your partner that you care for them and that you are happy you are together.

Clear the air

Avoid waiting till you are both fighting to bring up grievances. This only makes them become blown out of proportion. Make it a priority about once a week to ask your spouse if there is anything you have done to cause distance between you. It's important that both parties in a marriage know that they are interested in one another's feelings, even if they may cause an upset.

Throw away the score sheet

Many couples are not aware of it, but they unconsciously keep score of who does more chores, who get to hang out with their friends more, who has more money, who has more free time, etc. The sad thing is, couples tend to silently allow the resentment from these tallies to build up, which then negatively impacts many aspects of the marriage. Marriage is a team sport, if someone *is* winning, you are both losing. Throw out that silent score sheet and mentally keep shredding it till it becomes a habit *not* to keep score.

Apologize already

"I'm sorry" tends to be a heck of a lot harder to say than "I love you." No one likes admitting when they are in the wrong and at times, an apology can feel a lot like an admittance of defeat. No one is able to be right all the time. Your relationship with your spouse is much more important than being right. If you realize that the fight you are having is stupid and doesn't play a role in the bigger picture of things, learn to suck up your pride and say you are sorry. Your marriage should mean more to you than winning an argument.

Respect your spouse's time

There are many times that you ask your spouse to do something and months go by without lifting a finger to do it. Resentment builds drastically, which is no fun for either party. Instead, practice asking for what you want at a time that your spouse is able to do it for you. Asking for them to do things at more opportune times aids in a successful marriage because it shows them that you respect their time and are paying attention to their wants and needs as well.

Change the way your spouse sees you

In a marriage, you and your spouse are going to see many sides of one another. Human beings are naturally visual creatures. While this is part of sharing a life together, it can be quite helpful on occasion to portray yourself in a certain light. For instance, a woman could ask their husband to choose their lingerie before heading to bed. These little quirks help to tease one another, making them think about what their spouse is wearing *all* day so that they are anxious to come home.

Take initiative

Intimacy often times takes a backseat when it comes to living in the busy world the majority of us reside in today. But it is irresponsible for one or both spouses to wait for the other to make a move. Be spontaneous and give them a passionate kiss or bring home flowers and a delicious dessert. This will show your partner that you are physically, emotionally and mentally into them, even after all this time. Both of you will reap the rewards too!

Compare calendars

Check in with your partner each morning to see what is on their agenda for the day. This may seem very unromantic, but it helps to keep you both on the same page, even while you are apart. It also gives you the opportunity to check up on them later in the day, to encourage and support them. Everyone genuinely appreciates knowing that someone loves them enough to think about them during the course of their own busy days.

Pick connection over communication

Communication in 2018 happens largely over texting and email. Unfortunately, this provides couples with a lot of instant gratification, which can boil down conversations being boringly about daily tasks, scheduling, and other logistics. It can feel a lot like the trading of shifts. You should strive to put more connection in your communication by balancing your outbox. For each "to-do" reminder you send your spouse, make sure you also take the time to send a connecting text, such as a photo of a happy memory you share or something like, "You make me so happy!" You could even go as far as sending a slightly flirty note that builds their anticipation.

CHAPTER 7

LEARNING THE ACT OF FORGIVENESS

Many of us equate the act of forgiving with a warm feeling, but it is actually the opposite. Forgiveness, especially when it comes to someone you love, can be painful. While it may sound great as it comes out verbally, it makes people struggle with hypocrisy on the inside. It makes us become plagued with an abyss of resentment and bitterness and should not be viewed as a lip service.

Feelings that are left unchecked will find a way to become verbally, mentally, emotionally, and even physically murderous. Forgiveness is not about simply forgetting about an offense or choosing to inflict a price for the offense.

It can be challenging to forgive someone that you thought would never hurt you in the first place. But you must learn to forgive in order to keep the marriage you are part of alive. Forgiving and letting go of the past is a vital tool to a healthy marital relationship. It also plays an important part in keeping yourself healthy emotionally as well.

You are inevitably wasting you and your partner's time and energy if you hold on to anger, insensitivity, betrayals, annoyances, old hurts, and disappointments. The prolonged nursing of a perceived hurt will eventually turn into bitterness and a hate that is difficult to rid yourself of. In other words, a lack of forgiveness can wear you down, which in turn, wears out the marriage. Resentment will gain momentum over time and take chips out of your marriage's foundation.

How to Forgive Your Spouse

- Be patient with yourself, forgiveness takes time. No need to hurry the process along.

- Forgiving your spouse does not mean you condone their behavior that hurt you.

- Accept the fact that you may not know the reason for your partner's mistake and terrible behavior.

- Do not plan to seek out retribution or revenge of any kind. If you are always putting energy to get even with them, this is just extending the pain they have caused. Plus, it will not make you feel any better.

- Do not continuously throw the mistakes of your spouse at them later on. You should also not use their errors as ammunition against them in future arguments.

- When the images of hurt or betrayal come to mind, think of a place that calms your mind or do something that distracts you from dwelling on these negative thoughts.

- Make the decision to forgive your spouse consciously.

- Be receptive and open to the act of giving forgiveness.

Asking for Forgiveness from Your Spouse

- Make a verbal apology that comes from your heart. This will also include a plan of action that you should perform in order to make things right again.

- Be patient with the partner you hurt. Forgiveness takes time, and you should not dismiss how your spouse feels about the betrayal you caused or tell them to "get over it."

- Be open to making amends with your spouse.

- Accept the consequences of your actions that created the hurt.

- Make a commitment to not hurt your partner in the same way in the future again.

- Show true remorse for the pain you have caused your spouse.

Why Marriages *Need* Forgiveness

All close relationships in life rely on forgiveness to thrive. We are all human beings and no matter how hard we try, inevitably make mistakes from time to time. We all have bad and grumpy days, and we sometimes say things we do not mean. Everyone deserves to forgive and be forgiven. No matter how strong a marriage is, it cannot be sustained without forgiveness long term. Why you might find it challenging to forgive your spouse, it is crucial for you to do so if you want your marriage to move forward.

CHAPTER 8

RESTORING BROKEN TRUST

All marriages will go through difficult times thanks to trust being broken. In fact, the core of many problems within marriages occurs because of a breach of trust. The strength of marital relations requires a strong and trusting bond, which is why it is so vital to rebuild it when it does become damaged. If you find that your marriage is suffering from a lack of trust, this chapter is a must-read.

Take responsibility over your actions

If you are the one that is responsible for breaking the trust in your marriage, own your actions and apologize for them. Taking responsibility if the first step to seek out forgiveness and state your commitment to do whatever you have to in order to restore it.

If you are the one that must offer forgiveness, do not make excuses for your spouse's behavior, but be willing to take responsibility for any actions that you did that might have contributed to the breakdown of your relationship. Remember that forgiving does not instantly fix everything.

Forgiveness might occur quickly, but trust is restored slowly

Trust and forgiveness are two wildly different things. When you are wronged by your partner, you should learn to forgive them as quickly as possible. On the other hand, you should give your trust gradually over time. Forgiveness can be given, but trust can only be earned. Forgiveness is the first step in paving the way to restoring trust.

Do not retaliate

It is natural when you have been wronged by anyone to feel the urge to punish the person who hurt you. But you should do your best to fight the temptation to use their offenses as ammunition in the future. Do not constantly hold negative things over your spouse's head. While you may want them to feel the pain that they have caused you, it only is damaging the trust between the two of you even more. Holding grudges is like drinking poison and hoping that the other person dies. Discuss clear guidelines to how you want the trust to be restored, but you should never punish the other person for making a mistake.

Consistency is key

While you and your partner are undergoing the process of rebuilding trust, you both must do your best to be consistent in both what you say *and* do. This is an important part of bringing security. There are sadly no shortcuts to restoring the trust that has been lost.

Be willing to give up some freedoms temporarily

Just like when you break your arm, it must be put into a cast in order to restrict movement to allow it time to heal. The same goes for broken trust in that you both must be willing to give up freedoms and accept restrictions to allow the time you both need to mend. This can be pretty uncomfortable, but it is crucial. Both parties should be willing to put away their pride to do whatever necessary to rebuild trust. This may mean putting a filter on your electronic devices, putting a tracking app on your phones, giving yourselves a curfew, or anything else that provides reassurances to one another.

No secrets

Secrets are as dangerous as lying in marriages. Secrecy is the ultimate enemy of intimacy. When you get married, you must be willing to provide one another a master key to one another's lives. Don't have a conversation with your spouse that you don't want them to hear, don't look at websites you wouldn't want them to see or go somewhere you don't want them knowing about. Transparency is crucial to trust building.

Surround yourself with positive influences

If you constantly hang out with people that are untrustworthy, it is understandable if your partner finds it harder to trust you and your judgment. Learn to be intentional about the people you choose to hang out with, especially when you are married. Choose to spend your time out-side of your marriage with a small and trusted group of individuals who do not tempt you to act upon things that could further hurt your relationship.

Refuse to fall back into the same behavior

When there has been a breach of trust in specific areas, it can be easier for the spouse who was wronged to think that their partner might be a repeat offender. As human beings, we are all a work in progress, but you must real-ize that when you make bad decisions in repeated nega-tive areas, you reopen old wounds, which makes it much more difficult to rebuild trust. Do everything you can to not fall into a vicious cycle of empty apologies and mak-ing empty promises. Take initiative to change your over-all behavior in order to improve your marriage.

Keep moving forward

A big part of the reason why many marriages do not last is that one or both partners give up when the going gets rough. You must commit to love one another no matter what life brings the two of you. Do not lose hope, no matter how much your marriage might be struggling.

CHAPTER 9

GETTING OVER THE PAST TO REKINDLE YOUR MARRIAGE

One of the biggest desires married couples have is to stay together forever within a healthy, happy, and loving relationship. But holding on to past can hurt not only the wronged spouse but the entire marriage.

It is natural to feel betrayed and have a loss of trust in your partner when they hurt you. Once you have been hurt multiple times, your emotions can close up, and your heart can turn slightly to stone. This shuts down the ability to be close, both verbally and sexually. This means that your spouse becomes more of a roommate than an intimate partner.

To recapture the love that your marriage once had and to restore happiness, here are some steps to follow to get back to the way things were.

Identify the hurt

Step back in time to the first hurt and remember the way you reacted; did you brush it off, attempt to talk to your spouse or did you just shut down and cry? Did you feel understood and heard? Once you have reminisced about your first hurt, trace your steps back and see if the first hurt is similar to the others afterward. This will help you to clarify how you feel and provide you with a place to start to talk about your feelings with your spouse.

Sit down and talk

Invite your spouse to talk with you by letting them know that even though the first time they hurt you seemed small, it has grown bigger and you have since not let it go. By taking the time to acknowledge your feelings and letting them have a chance to take it seriously, you are giving yourself a first step to let go of the pain that haunts you, which enables you to move forward.

Listen

Make it a practice to take turns talking to one another. Have two monologues instead of a dialogue. Learn the importance of putting your feelings to the side to allow your partner to speak. Do not interrupt them and really attempt to step into their shoes. Then switch roles. This will give you both a chance to feel heard. You will hear even the smallest things differently when you choose to consciously listen, which allows the both of you to create a new perspective.

Be present and check in

Once you have listened to one another, you are now at the present time, which allows you to really think of the hurts you need to let go. Hurt usually stems directly from misunderstanding and miscommunication. Hurt makes us forget to check in with your spouse and hear them correctly. Checking in helps you to restore the trust with your partner. Talking to one another without blame can give you a chance to resolve painful feelings and not carry them with you to the future. This way you both have a much better chance of resolving those painful re-sentments and remain present at all times.

Create a plan to keep your marriage current

After you have discussed your hurts and worries with your spouse, you will both

feel understood and listened to. For the future, make an agreement to talk as soon as hurt happens. Don't allow hurt to stack on top of one another.

Prove that change has occurred

Often times, both spouses are responsible for hurting one another. This means that it is vital that both of you go out of your way to prove to one another that you have changed. This means acquiring the skill of patience. When you both have genuinely overcome your behavior, then patience is needed to change the attitude towards the healing process.

Patience is a virtue

The awakening to hurt from both parties can dredge up many negative feelings. When it comes to healing, it takes time to think about and process the things that have occurred. Through patience, your spouse will come to realize that making changes goes way beyond how they act towards you. You must also allow yourself time to heal from the past. It is a natural process that cannot be rushed.

Awareness

There will finally come a day that you realize that your spouse has grown from the consequences of their actions. Guards still remain up as the powers of observation are heightened. This allows both parties to regain the hope they need as they can see new things coming upon the horizon. Expected behaviors diminish, and new, more loving ones take their place. Respect and trust are allowed to grow rapidly. Do not rush this step, however, Let it grow and unravel as it does. Make sure you are still making observations that allow you to see the trust between you and your spouse grow.

CHAPTER 10

LEARNING TO LOVE YOURSELF AGAIN

One of the hardest things to grasp about fixing marriages is the blatant fact that it initially begins with *you*. While some of the resentment and emptiness you feel may be partially your spouse's fault, much of it stems from your inner self. Self-abandonment instills the negative feelings that make resentment in the marriage grow. Dysfunctional marriages will continuously grow despite your efforts to patch things up with your spouse. In order to get down to the nitty-gritty of what might be ruining your marriage, it might be time to look at yourself in the mirror.

You might be abandoning yourself if you are:

- Making your partner feel responsible for how you feel

- Turning to addictions to numb negative feelings

- Judging yourself

- Ignoring how you feel by honing in on what is happening in your head rather than your body

Developing Self-Love in a Marriage

Learning to love yourself is a life-long and ongoing process. Even marriages that have a healthy amount of self-love could have more. Here is how to maintain self-love within your marriage!

Maintain independence and space

You should never allow your marriage to absorb your entire identity. You should never find yourself losing your entire self-worth and what makes you, you. In order to keep your marriage healthy, you need to keep your own friends, interests, and rituals. Spend a healthy allotment of time doing the things that you find to nurture your soul.

You are the master of your happiness

No matter how hard they try, your spouse cannot make you happy. You are the only one that is solely in charge of your happiness. It is not anyone else's responsibility but your own. If you rely on your spouse for contentment, you will literally drain the space that is between you.

Self-love is a habit you must be willing to practice over time. You must learn to adopt the mindset that happiness is a choice you make, which will then give you the power to cultivate happiness for yourself. This is much easier said than done, especially if you are one that allows your happiness to be dictated by others.

Choose to be present and don't just wait for the perfect moment to be happy. Quiet those negative thoughts and decide to be happy at the moment instead! Act on little things that make you happy by embracing the daily moments. Nurturing yourself by meditating or drinking a cup of tea will help to quiet the mind and allow you to be totally present at the moment and enjoy your days thoroughly.

You also need to make it a priority to work through the baggage from your past, for it is only then you will feel lighter, and it will be much easier to choose happiness. Working through pain is an ongoing process, but you should not let it hold you back from being yourself and finding contentment.

See yourself how your partner sees you

Those that are insecure strongly struggle to see what is good about themselves and are very dismissive of the things that their spouse sees in them. Ask your partner what they see in you and what they love about you. In fact, this can be a great and fun exercise for a date night. Write a list of 15-20 things that you love about one another and take turns reading them.

This will help you to internalize that you are an amazing person and truly believe it each day. The things that you are the most critical about are more than likely the pieces of you that your spouse thoroughly enjoys!

Don't become disheartened by your flaws

All people have flaws, it is what makes us who we are. But you need to recognize that relationships have a funny way of holding a mirror right up to those flaws. Things you have just learned to live with may irritate your spouse. While some flaws can easily be ignored, others need to be worked through. Do not be afraid to expose your flaws, for it is a natural part of a healthy relationship. Your flaws do not make you unlovable.

Forgive yourself

Holding grudges against yourself can majorly put a roadblock up against loving yourself. Do not beat yourself up over past actions.

Love is an action, not a feeling

Love is something that we consciously choose to do, not just something that we feel. While this is commonly said about choosing one another, it is something we forget when it comes to loving ourselves. Make it a priority to schedule "you time" each and every day. This is important, for you put yourself first, above any other priorities and commitments. Do something simple you enjoy! While one session at first will not make a huge difference, you will be surprised at how the creation of a self-love ritual will make a positive impact over time, and will provide great changes to your marriage as well!

CONCLUSION

I want to congratulate you for making it to the end of the *Marriage Counseling Book: How to Deal with "I Don't Love You."*

I hope that the contents of this book have helped you to learn new things about rebuilding your marriage from the rubble that life has left you and your beloved spouse with. Everyone deserves a long-lasting and loving marriage till death separates them physically. As you have read and very well know, life gets in the way more often than we think. But there are many things you both can do to reimplement the love and respect you once had for one another before life started wearing down your relationship.

That said, I hope that this book will help you to repave a positive path in getting your marriage and relationship with your spouse back on track! It will not happen overnight, but if each of you is dedicated enough to want to rekindle that flame and rebuild a broken home, please feel free to return to the pages of this book time and time again till you both are healed from the past and can go forward in life stronger than before.

The next step is to put the information from this book to the test within your crumbling marriage. Even if your relationship with your partner is just not as great as you would like it to be, take the steps in this book to counteract negative results now before it becomes a bigger mess than you know what to do with!

If you found this book useful in any way, please take a moment to head to Amazon and leave a review. It is always appreciated!

Description

It is time to put the sugar coating, empty promises, and spewing of hateful words to your beloved spouse aside. You are using Dr. Google to search for ways to fix your broken marriage, which I am thankful that your search led you to reading this description.

Despite popular belief, there are many ways that you can go to fix a marriage that seems lost and pointless to be in. We all tend to lose our way once the honeymoon phase wears off, which is the core in which many marital problems grow. Whether you have been unhappy within your partnership for a long time now or you are just starting to see red flags and have doubts, this book is a one-stop resource for all aspects of marriage, even the pieces you wish you could simply lock away.

No one deserves to live their life cautiously stepping around their partner in fear of making things worse. This is the most awful way to live! Within the chapters of this book you will find:

- The reasons that marriages are in such turmoil in today's world

- Signs that your marriage might be taking a turn for the wort

- How to break off affairs and rebuild after their devastation

- Out of the box methods to fix your marriage

- Ways to bring love and passion back into your marriage

- How to learn to forgive

- Learning to rebuild a marriage with broken trust

- How to get over the past to move forward

- Learning to love yourself again

- And more!

Whether you can admit it or not, a marriage takes the dedication, love, compassion, and trust of *two* people. If your marriage is privy to more bad times than good, it is about time that you start to think of your partner and the marriage you are both in together differently. It is only then that you can both mend and rebuild the crumbling foundation that could cause further emotional damage in the near future.

What are you waiting for? Both you and your partner are together for a reason, right? Why give something as sacred as a marriage up just because of issues that can be resolved if you are willing to work hard to find that flame between the two of you once again?